BASEBALL LEAGUE LOGOS

COLORING BOOK

THIS BOOK BELONGS TO:

NEW YORK YANKEES

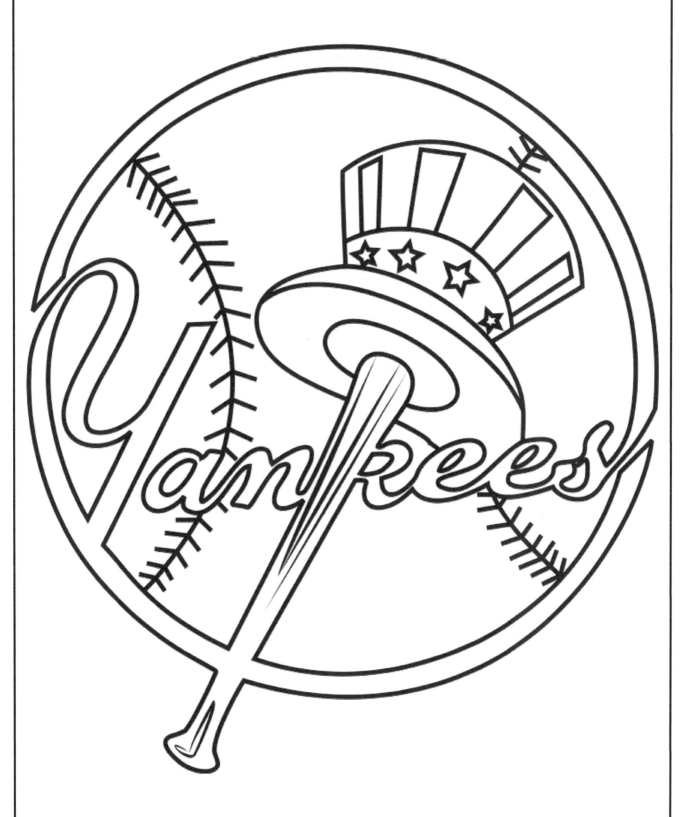

ST LOUIS CARDINALS

WASHINGTON NATIONALS

TEXAS RANGERS

TORONTO BLUE JAYS

TAMPA BAY RAYS

SEATTLE MARINERS

SAN FRANCISCO GIANTS

SAN DIEGO PADRES

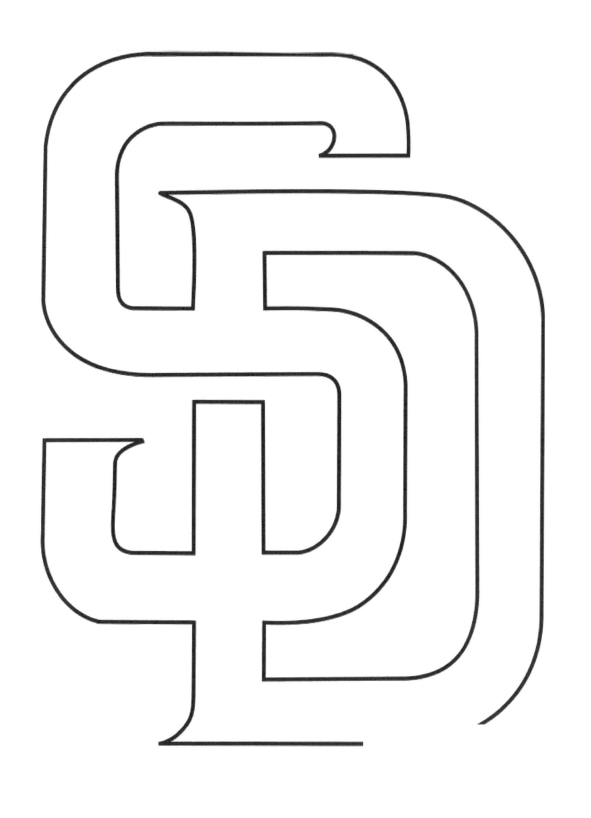

PITTSBURGH PIRATES

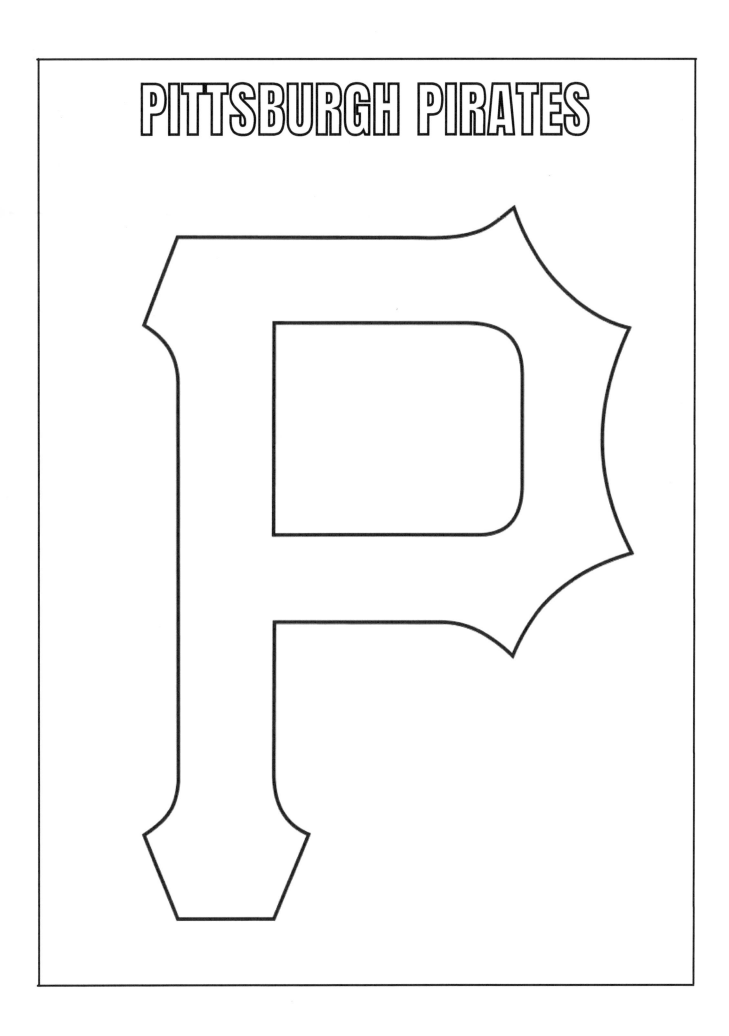

PHILADELPHIA PHILLIES

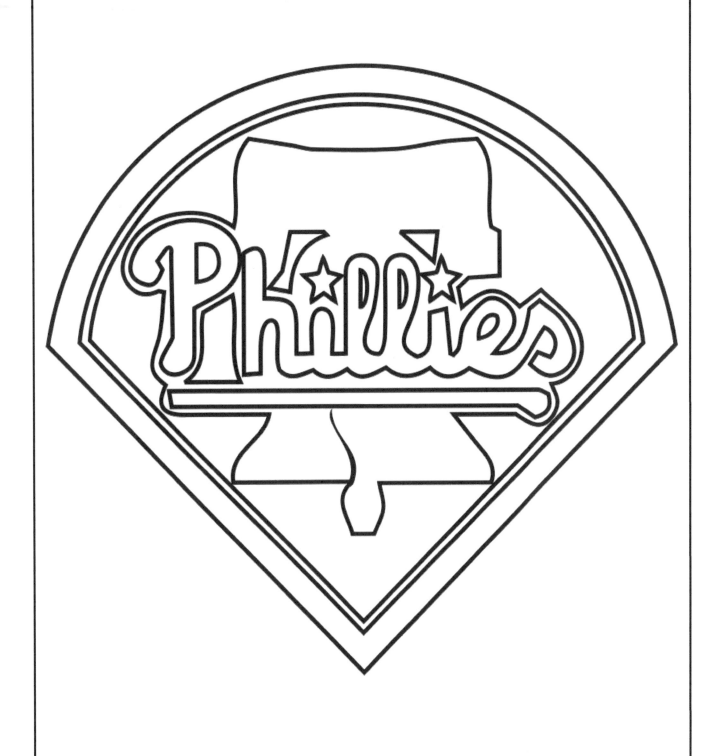

OAKLAND ATHLETICS

NEW YORK METS

MINNESOTA TWINS

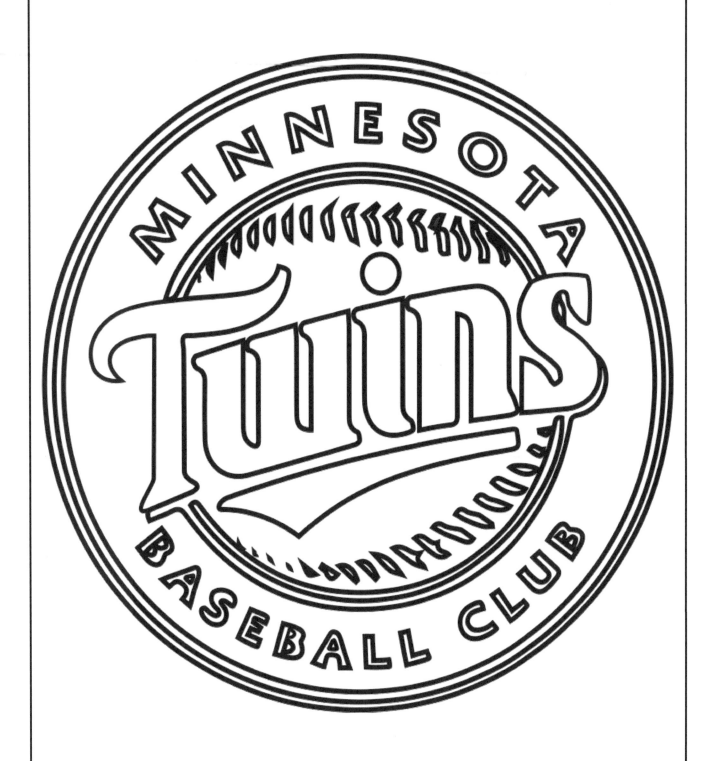

MILWAUKEE BREWERS

LOS ANGELES DODGERS

LOS ANGELES ANGELS OF ANAHEIM

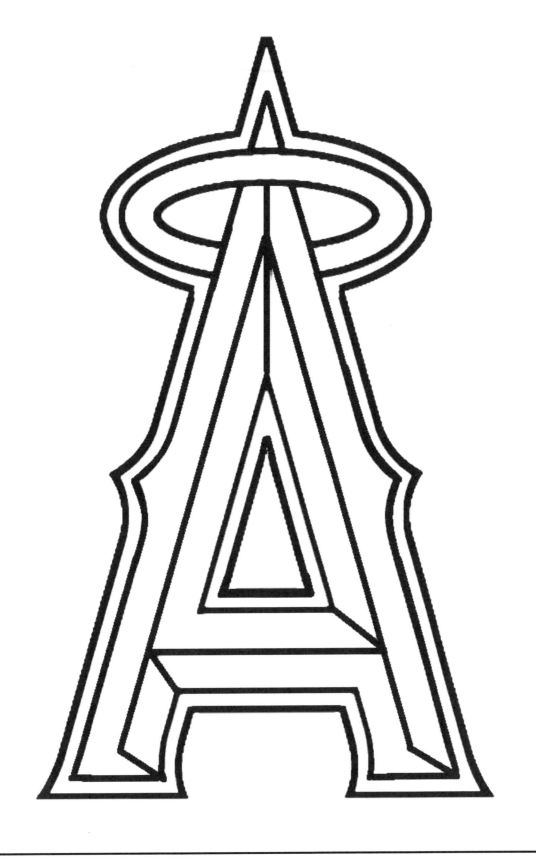

KANSAS CITY ROYALS

Royals

HOUSTON ASTROS

DETROIT TIGERS

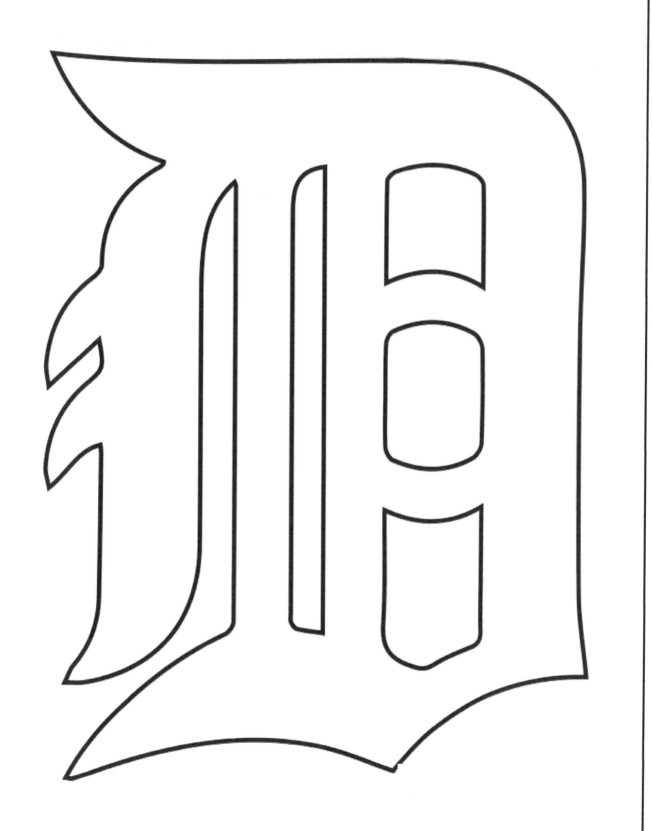

COLORADO ROCKIES

CLEVELAND INDIANS

CINCINNATI REDS

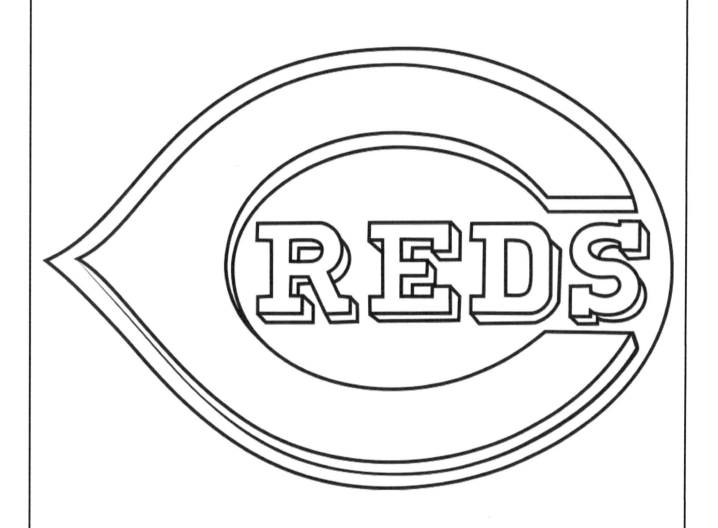

CHICAGO WHITE SOX

CHICAGO CUBS

BOSTON RED SOX

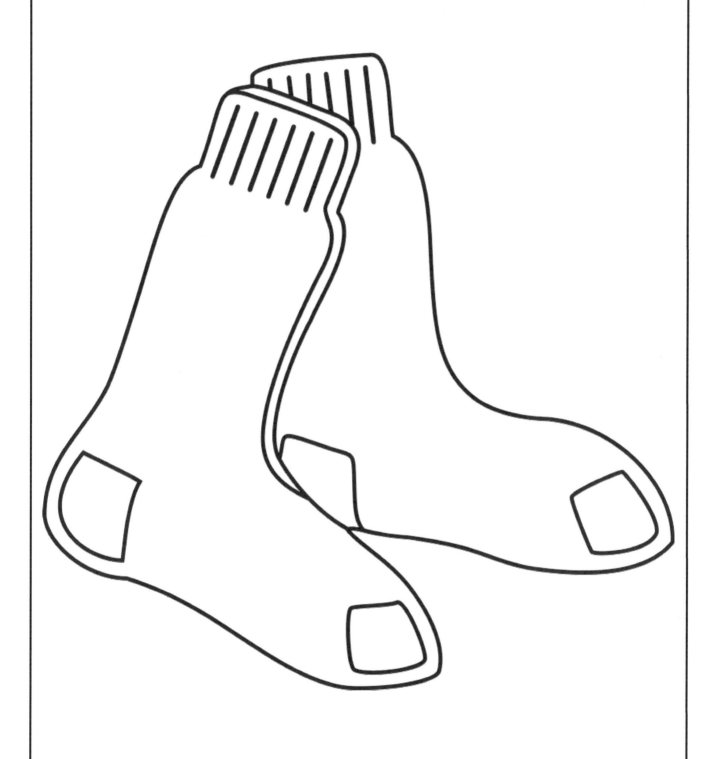

BALTIMORE ORIOLES

ATLANTA BRAVES

ARIZONA DIAMONDBACKS

Made in United States
Troutdale, OR
12/16/2023

15912043R00040